ANTARCTIC
Survival

Robert Swan
Leader of the 'In the Footsteps of Scott' Antarctic Expedition

Researcher — Rupert Summerson

Macdonald

Contents

Antarctic Explorers

I went to Antarctica in 1985 because I had long dreamed of walking to the South Pole in the footsteps of Captain Scott. I wanted to know what it felt like to be hundreds of kilometres from any other people, with only what I could pull behind me on a sledge to keep me alive in the most hostile conditions on Earth. But also, I wanted to draw everyone's attention to the importance of Antarctica. Unlike every other bit of land in the world, no person or country owns it — rather, we all do, and that means you, too.

In 1066, when William the Conqueror won the Battle of Hastings, no one had ever seen Antarctica. Although the ancient Greeks had thought enough about their world to wonder what lay to the far south and to give a name to it, a journey from Greece to Italy was enough to tax their navigation skills to the limit. In 1492 Christopher Columbus discovered America, and in 1578 Francis Drake sailed round the southern tip of South America, but still no one had found what lay farther south. All sorts of wild guesses were made as to what was there. Then, in 1773 James Cook became the first person to cross the Antarctic Circle (nearly 3000 kilometres from the South Pole), but try as hard as he could, masses of pack-ice prevented him from going any farther south. It was not until 1820 that anyone discovered land; Thaddeus von Bellingshausen, a Russian, and William Smith both saw bits of what is now known to be the Antarctic continent.

Previous page: A painting of Ross' ship, Erebus, in front of Mount Erebus in the Antarctic, on 28 January 1841. Ross named the mountain after the ship. The ship on the right is the Terror.

James Clarke Ross, one of Britain's greatest polar explorers.

Carsten Borchgrevink was possibly the first person to set foot on the Antarctic continent.

The greatest of all 19th century explorers must be James Ross who made new discoveries of huge tracts of coastline and pointed the way to reaching the South Pole. In honour of his achievements he now has two islands, a sea and an ice shelf named after him, all of which he discovered. The first person to stay any time in Antarctica was Carsten Borchgrevink, whose ship left his expedition to spend the winter of 1899 on the mainland. By now it had become clear that no people had ever lived in Antarctica.

The 20th century
Captain Robert Scott first went to the Antarctic in 1902, staying there through two winters until 1904. In 1903, he and two companions made the first attempt to reach the South Pole which was about 1500 kilometres from their ship. In 1909, Ernest Shackleton, who had been with Scott in 1902, made another attempt, but he too had to turn back – only 178 kilometres short of the Pole.

But it was Roald Amundsen, the Norwegian explorer, and his four companions who were the first to the Pole in December 1911. Captain Scott, who was back with his second expedition, and his four companions arrived at the Pole a month after Amundsen, but all five died on the way back to the coast. Petty Officer Edgar Evans died after a fall. Captain Lawrence Oates sacrificed himself after he had become badly frost-bitten and exhausted, rather than become a burden on the others. Scott, Wilson and Bowers died together in their tent when a blizzard prevented them reaching their depot of food and fuel – only 18 kilometres away.

Captain and Mrs Scott on the 'Terra Nova' in Lyttelton harbour, New Zealand. After Scott's death, Kathleen Scott went on to pursue a career as a sculptor.

Above: Sir Ernest Shackleton, taken on the 'Endurance' expedition, his third to the Antarctic. **Below:** Roald Amundsen, the Norwegian explorer who led the first expedition to reach the South Pole.

Since then, interest in Antarctica has gone up and down. Expeditions have come and gone and the blank spaces on the maps have gradually been filled in. Recently, there has been a lot more interest because the Antarctic Treaty, which controls what goes on there, is soon to be reviewed. Up till now, those countries which have signed the Treaty, and so declared an interest in the Antarctic, have made the rules. Any other countries who want to have a say in how the Treaty is revised are quickly joining 'the club' of Antarctic nations. There are now 31 member nations. The Antarctic Treaty, as well as protecting Antarctica peacefully, has been an example of international co-operation. One of the greatest fears is that if the Treaty is changed, it will open the way to disputes, exploitation and destruction of the wildlife.

Many people, however, want to leave the Antarctic exactly as it is, with nobody being allowed to drill for oil or quarry for minerals. The ocean around Antarctica is rich in wildlife: birds, seals and whales all live there in abundance – it may seem peculiar, but the icy seawater there is rich in food for these animals. Living conditions are very harsh and too much intrusion by people could destroy the animals' habitat. At the moment, no one is allowed to drill or quarry. The Antarctic Treaty only allows peaceful scientific activity, but all that could change . . .

Reaching Antarctica

My first view of the continent which had been in my dreams for so long was of the coast of Graham Land. I was with the British Antarctic Survey (BAS), a government scientific research organisation, on my first visit to Antarctica in 1980. The great rocky cliffs with their thick caps of ice, glowing orangey-pink in the late evening sun, made me think of them as ranks of soldiers. They were the last defences of the continent that had remained hidden for so long.

Anyone who goes to Antarctica must be fully equipped to cope with the rigours of the climate. You must take all your own food, your own hut, lots of warm clothing, and, if you want electricity, your own generator to make it. When we arrived, all we found was a cold, icy, empty beach; exactly the same as Captain Scott found in 1911.

First of all you have to get there, and most people go by ship as they have to transport so much equipment. Any old ship will not do; it has to be specially strengthened against being crushed by the pack-ice which surrounds Antarctica.

Our expedition left Britain in November 1984 in our own ship, the Southern Quest. Amongst the supplies we had on board were: 500 tins of baked beans, over half a tonne of flour, 150 tubes of toothpaste, 250 bottles of tomato ketchup, nearly 350 kilos of sugar, and much more. This was food not only for the ship's crew during the voyage to Anarctica and back, but also for the five of us staying, including the three members of the party going to the South Pole. In total we had over 50 tonnes of supplies, including the hut.

Like Captain Scott we sailed from London to Cardiff to pick up some coal, then on to Cape Town, South Africa and Lyttelton in New Zealand, before heading south into the pack-ice. From Lyttelton, it took 10 days to reach Cape Evans, on Ross Island, where we were going to set up our base, right next to Captain Scott's hut from his second expedition.

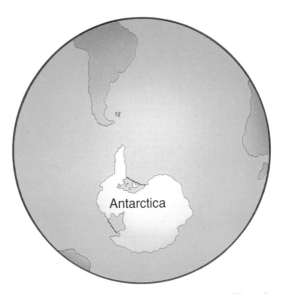

The position of Antarctica on the globe. The closest countries are Chile, Argentina, South Africa and New Zealand.

We had to be quick unloading all our stores because the Antarctic summer is short and the sea thaws for only a short time before it starts to re-freeze. Because the southern hemisphere seasons are the opposite of those in the northern hemisphere, we arrived at Cape Evans at the height of summer, on 8 February. Even so, the temperature was −12°C!

The first thing we had to do once we had everything ashore was to build our hut. It came in pre-fabricated sections, so after finding a level space well above the highest tide we began to build it. Four days later it was up.

Opposite: The Southern Quest off Cape Evans, with the mountains of Victoria Land to the west behind.

Stores being unloaded off the Southern Quest, to be taken ashore on the pontoon. Once ashore, many of the supplies were stacked in lines near the site where the hut was to be built.

Visiting neighbours

Our nearest neighbours were at the American base, called McMurdo, 27 kilometres to the west. In the summer this is a small town of some 2000 scientists, assistants, administrators, pilots and maintenance teams. By now, though, most had gone back to the USA for the winter, leaving only a 'skeleton' staff to keep the place ticking over. Even then there were still over 80 people there, by far the largest base in Antarctica. I was anxious to visit McMurdo and the nearby Scott Base as soon as possible to make contact and introduce ourselves. Also, McMurdo is built all round the hut Captain Scott built during his first expedition in 1902, and I wanted to see that, too. So as soon as we had things sorted out at Cape Evans, we re-embarked on the Southern Quest and sailed round to McMurdo. It only took a couple of hours and we were soon tied up alongside the ice wharf there.

The size of McMurdo astonished us – it really did seem like a small town, with streets and street-lights, a cinema and a chapel. The Americans were very friendly and showed us round, and we even had Coca-Cola and ice-cream! We were also impressed by the size of Scott's hut from his 1902–1904 expedition. The members actually spent two winters in their ship, the Discovery, and the hut was only used as a refuge. (The Discovery is now in Dundee, Scotland, undergoing restoration).

The American base, McMurdo, at night. It is so big it even has street-lights!

Just over the hill behind McMurdo is New Zealand's base, Scott Base. This is much smaller than McMurdo and there were only 14 people wintering there. New Zealand is a lot smaller country than the USA and so can only afford a small base. We found the 'Kiwis' very friendly and hospitable also, and we used their post office. Also at Scott Base are some huskies. Nowadays explorers use vehicles to get about, but Scott Base and a few others still keep huskies as a reminder that most of the early exploration of Antarctica was done with teams of these splendid dogs pulling the explorers' sledges.

A team of huskies about to leave Scott Base.

Left behind

On 23 February the ship finally departed for warmer climes. There were five of us on that beach when the ship disappeared over the horizon: Roger Mear, first-class mountaineer and a friend from my BAS days – it was his expertise that would get us to the Pole; Gareth Wood, climbing instructor, who designed the base; Doctor Michael Stroud, another ex-BAS man – as well as look after us medically he would do some research on us; Captain John Tolson, ex-BAS ship's Mate, who would make the film of the expedition.

The last thing to do to the hut was to anchor it to the ground by steel cables thrown over the roof. Captain Scott's expedition had recorded windspeeds of 135 kilometres per hour and we did not want to be blown into the sea. Then we had all the stores to arrange in lines outside and to record what was in each dump. They all had to be marked because we quite expected that some or maybe all of them would be buried by the winter snowfalls. The dumps were all carefully positioned so that snowdrifts building up behind a line would not bury the one next to it.

Scott's hut was only 200 metres from ours, so as soon as we had built our own we went to visit his. It was not quite as he had left it because a party from one of Sir Ernest Shackleton's expeditions had lived there several years later, but we could still sense that this was Scott's hut. It had a ghostly atmosphere as if Scott and his men had just left. The very dry, cold climate preserves things remarkably and all his supplies on the shelves still had their labels on. There were tins of Lyle's syrup, Heinz baked beans and Colman's mustard. The labels look old-fashioned but you can still find many of the products on the shelves in supermarkets today. The atmosphere was so eery that no one could bear to stay overnight.

The five winterers, taken just before the ship left. Left to right: John Tolson (film-maker), Gareth Wood (Base commander), me, Michael Stroud (doctor), Roger Mear (co-leader).

Hut Life

As we approached North Bay on our way back from McMurdo I was struck by how small our hut was compared to the places we had just visited. And yet here was all we needed to live in great comfort, in warmth and security for as long as our food and fuel lasted. There was enough for two years and then we would have to start living off the land. It should be possible to survive for a further year as long as there are seals and penguins about. One of Scott's parties had survived in an ice cave for a winter, supplementing their meagre rations with seals and penguins and cooking on an improvised stove using seal blubber as fuel. They all survived, but only just.

Plan of the downstairs of our hut.

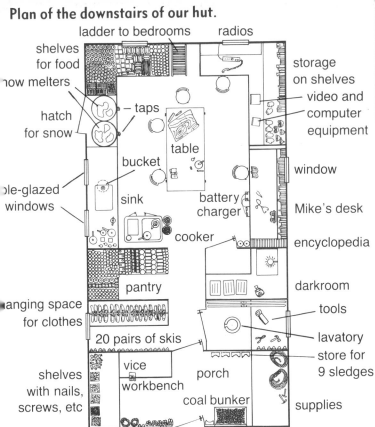

Labels on the plan:
- shelves for food
- snow melters
- hatch for snow
- ble-glazed windows
- ladder to bedrooms
- radios
- taps
- table
- bucket
- sink
- battery charger
- cooker
- pantry
- anging space for clothes
- 20 pairs of skis
- shelves with nails, screws, etc
- vice workbench
- porch
- coal bunker
- shoes, ice axes, rope
- storage on shelves
- video and computer equipment
- window
- Mike's desk
- encyclopedia
- darkroom
- tools
- lavatory
- store for 9 sledges
- supplies

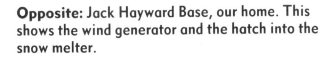

Opposite: Jack Hayward Base, our home. This shows the wind generator and the hatch into the snow melter.

John by the cooker inside our hut. The bucket under the sink is instead of a drain-pipe.

We called our base after Sir Jack Hayward, one of the expedition's benefactors. We entered it through the porch where we stored our sledges and skis. We had to keep them indoors otherwise the wind would have blown them away and covered them with snow and then they would have been lost. Also in the porch was a work-bench with a vice, and a box of coal which we kept stocked up from the sacks outside. We brought 16 tonnes of coal which, like Captain Scott, we were given in Cardiff, courtesy of British Coal.

From the porch, we went through the door into the hut itself. We hung up our outdoor clothes just inside the door. Opposite was a store-room which doubled as the lavatory — this was a chemical lavatory which had to be emptied periodically down the tide-crack into the sea. (A tide-crack is where the floating sea-ice meets the shore. The sea-ice goes up and down with the tides, so there is always a broken area which can be quite dangerous.) Next space along was the pantry where we kept a lot of food and anything which must not be allowed to freeze. If a bottle of tomato ketchup freezes it expands and breaks the bottle.

The living room

Next was the living room. Immediately on the left was the cooker which ran on coal and which also heated the hut. It was a specially modified Esse cooker, painted black to help radiate the heat. Straight in front was the dining table. Going round the room leftwards, next to the cooker was the kitchen sink. (Yes, we did take that too!) Next to that were the water tanks. We got water by melting snow; in the bottom of each tank was an immersion heater which kept the melt-water fairly warm. As long as there was still some warm water in the tank it melted any added snow quite efficiently. The snow was thrown in through a special hatch cut in the outside wall. At the bottom of each tank was a tap and these made do as kitchen tap, bathroom tap and clothes washing tap, all in one!

In the far left hand corner the wall was covered with shelves, all filled with food. Opposite the entrance was a ladder up to the bedrooms.

Next to the ladder, on the right, was Gareth's radio desk with all his books and spares. The radio was a high-frequency transmitter and receiver, and with it we were able to contact the

13

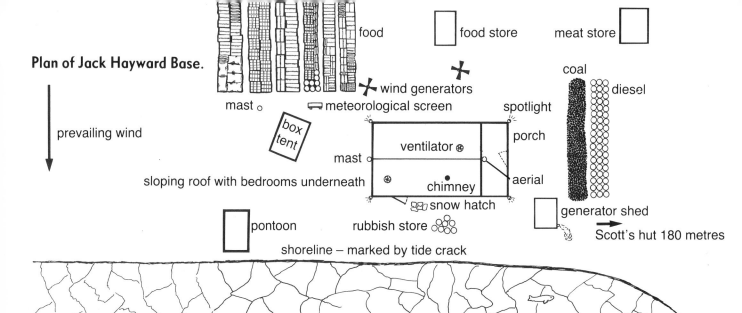

Plan of Jack Hayward Base.

food

food store

meat store

wind generators

coal

diesel

mast

meteorological screen

prevailing wind

box tent

spotlight

porch

ventilator

mast

aerial

sloping roof with bedrooms underneath

chimney

snow hatch

generator shed

pontoon

rubbish store

Scott's hut 180 metres

shoreline – marked by tide crack

Americans at McMurdo and the New Zealanders at Scott Base. In August we also managed to contact a friend at Rothera, a British base on the other side of the continent. The aerials were mounted outside, from time to time, when the wind had not blown them over!

Next to the radios was a desk with the video recorder and the computer. Even at Cape Evans we had the use of new technology. The computer was very useful for calculating amounts of supplies needed for the Polar journey. Roger also played chess with it but he wouldn't let on who used to win! Under the window in the right hand corner was Mike's desk and the apparatus he would use for tests on us, and so contribute to scientific research on the human body. Above was the complete Encylopedia Britannica which was frequently called upon to settle arguments. We're nearly back to where we started, and the only other thing was the darkroom. This must have been one of the few features our hut had in common with Scott's. Most of the photographs of Scott's last expedition were taken by Herbert Ponting, a world famous photographer, and many were developed in his darkroom at Cape Evans. Scott's hut was more open plan than ours, and a lot bigger because there were 28 men. Also, his was just a single storey – ours had an upstairs!

Upstairs

Going upstairs, above the ladder was a big window that opened outwards so we could get out in case of fire. There was also a hatch at the other end into the porch. Outside we kept a big box tent ready erected, with emergency supplies in it. If the hut was burnt down we could go and shelter in that. Fire is the greatest hazard to huts in the Antarctic.

We slept up there, under the roof. We each had the same amount of space and how we occupied it reflected the character of each person. For instance, my space was filled with cheerful chaos whilst Gareth's was neat and tidy. John's reflected his nautical background and was ship-shape. Mike's was like a doctor's hand-writing, and Roger's was spare and spartan. Additional space was used for storing personal kit which would not fit in the rooms.

The interior of Scott's hut. The cold, dry atmosphere preserves many things just as Scott left them.

Heating was no problem: hot air rises, and was assisted by some holes drilled in the ceiling over the cooker.

The hut itself was made of wood – to be precise a sandwich of two layers of wood with a thick layer of insulation material in between. The windows were all triple-glazed with the outer pane made of armour-plate glass to prevent it being broken by stones flung up by the wind.

Outside

That was everything inside the hut. Outside, opposite the front door, was the generator shed. Inside it was a small diesel generator which produced a 240 volt electricity supply. This was supplemented by two wind generators. There was no shortage of wind power in the Antarctic and rather than use expensive diesel, of which we had only a limited supply and which would pollute the lovely pure air, we used the wind generators as much as possible. Also outside were the dumps of coal, diesel drums, six dumps of food, and one of general equipment for which there was not room inside.

Passing the time

It would be hard to describe a typical day as each one was different. Some of us would get up early and some late, and the only meal that everyone sat down to together was supper. We took it in turns for one person to do the daily chores such as filling the generator, bringing in the coal and filling the water tanks and emptying the lavatory. He would also cook the supper. We baked bread once every other day, on average.

The chores necessary just to survive took up most of our time, particularly the job of ensuring that there was a supply of snow for the water tanks and a supply of fuel for melting the snow, and then emptying away waste water – we couldn't have drain pipes as they would have frozen up immediately. Imagine how often you pour away water in a day and you can see how much work we had to do!

When the weather was good, we could make short journeys as training for the walk to the Pole. But if the weather was bad, we would be stuck inside the hut for days on end. We did a lot of reading – books we'd always intended to read but had never had time to do it – and we each had our own specific jobs.

I was responsible for writing and typing newsletters for all our sponsors and supporters. The letters might not be delivered for months but at least I could write up our news at regular intervals. Roger took care of the navigation,

The Earth's axis is slightly tilted, so that as it travels round the Sun, some parts get more daylight than others. In December, the Antarctic is tilted towards the Sun and has daylight 24 hours a day. In June, the South Pole is in complete darkness.

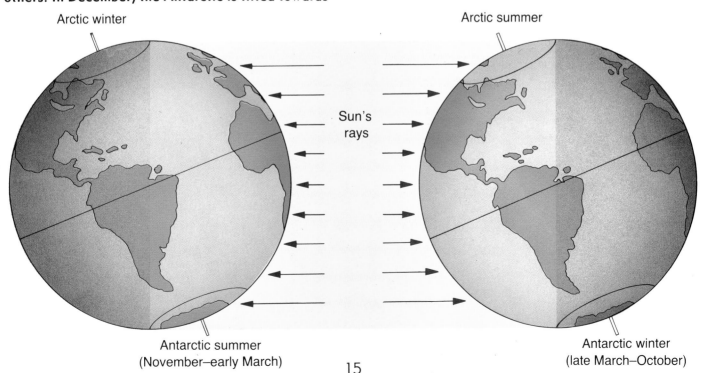

Arctic winter

Arctic summer

Sun's rays

Antarctic summer
(November–early March)

Antarctic winter
(late March–October)

working out routes and checking maps. Gareth was in charge of the radios, keeping us in touch with the outside world and seeing that the aerials were kept up, as they were often blown down. He was also in charge of the wind generator. John was keeping a film record of the whole expedition and, of course, there was a lot of equipment for that to be looked after. And Mike was doing tests and keeping records of our physical and mental state throughout the expedition.

As the days went by, winter came nearer. The Sun sank below the horizon for the last time on 12 April, but there was still plenty of twilight for two or three weeks after that. For quite some time, the twilight was accompanied by the most glorious colours in the northern sky.

The other tenants of Cape Evans all knew about the approach of winter, too. The Adelie penguins, visiting from their rookery at Cape Royds, were seen less and less frequently as they started their migration north. They were soon followed by the skuas. Good riddance to them! Every time anyone approaches them they soar off into the air and then proceed to dive-bomb you, sometimes clouting you with their feet. Only the Weddell seals stayed behind. These are big, grey

Adelie penguins in characteristic poses, and uncertain what to make of tinned fish!

slug-like animals which lie about on the beach, gently snoring and periodically scratching themselves with a delicately extended flipper. They are not afraid of humans, except when you inadvertently tread on one . . . but that is another story!

A Weddell seal waking up with a yawn and a scratch. Seals haul out of the water to sleep.

First Journeys

The autumn brought the real Antarctic blizzards and it was not long before the beach, briefly cleared of snow at the end of the summer, was pristine and white again. This brought a new, but not unexpected problem. The wind picked up snow from the beach and whirled it around, buffeting and blinding anyone outside. Unless he was in direct contact with a known landmark, he would soon be disorientated and lost even though he was only five metres from the hut. This happened to me while I was returning from Scott's hut to our own — only 200 metres away. I groped and fumbled my way about, getting more and more frightened. The same thing had happened to Surgeon Atkinson on Scott's expedition. They had found him eventually; he had wandered almost seven kilometres, and his hands were dreadfully frost-bitten. Fortunately, in a brief lull I saw the light on our hut, put there expressly for this purpose, and I blessed the advances in technology since Scott's day that had enabled us to put it there.

After our visit to McMurdo and Scott Base we decided to make the most of the good weather before winter arrived and explore more of our surroundings. We could not all go out at once as the hut should not be left unattended, so John and I stayed behind while Roger, Gareth and Mike set off to ski across Ross Island, taking in the two mountains of Erebus and Terror (named by James Ross after his ships). This was the first opportunity to test our clothing and equipment for the journey to the Pole.

Protective clothing

The body's first line of defence against the cold is, of course, clothing. The best insulation is, perhaps surprisingly, 'still air' and this is provided by the mass of fibres found in natural down and some artificial fibres, each curl of which retains a pocket of still air. Rather than have one thick layer of clothing, it has been found better to have several layers of thinner clothes, the layers trapping still air between them as well as within the layers. The outer layer has to be wind-proof. Also, having many layers makes it easier to prevent overheating and sweating by removing one or two layers. If it is very cold and you start sweating, the sweat will condense and freeze in the outer layers of clothing. Water is a good conductor of heat, which means that heat will escape quickly through sweat and ice, so it is important to keep dry. (Dirt has a similar effect.) One of the important features of our clothing was a water-proof layer to prevent our sweat getting into our down outer layer. It felt a bit like wearing a padded raincoat inside-out, but it was a lot warmer that way.

Previous page: Roger setting out to surprise the residents at McMurdo.

The layers of polar clothing:
a) Me in my underpants – bottom layer.
b) Roger in thermal underwear. This type does not absorb sweat – drier is warmer.
c) Roger in fibre-pile trousers and jacket.
d) Roger in salopettes.
e) Me in salopettes and down jacket – the top layer.

a

b

c

d

e

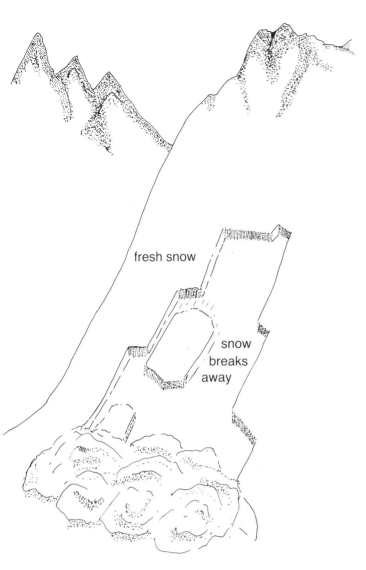

fresh snow

snow breaks away

The most common types of avalanche in the Antarctic happen after fresh snowfalls. Loose snow or whole slabs break away as the snow becomes too heavy for friction to hold it on the slope.

Mount Erebus and Mount Terror

Anyway, Roger, Gareth and Mike set out on 18 March. This is Gareth's account of the journey. 'The first stage was to pick a route through the rocks at the base of Mount Erebus. This was not too difficult as we were not pulling sledges but had all our equipment in rucksacks. Once beyond the rocks we had to watch out for crevasses, which are deep chasms in the ice, often camouflaged with snow.

The blizzards of the week before had laid a lot of fresh snow on the slopes of the mountains so once on the mountain we had to be very careful of avalanches. (An avalanche is a snow-slide, caused when the force of gravity overcomes the ability of the snow to stick to a slope. The slope has to be quite steep for it to happen, at least as steep as the steepest road in Britain. Dozens of people die in avalanches every year, including some on mountains in Britain, and we did not want to bring the expedition to an early close. The destructive power of a big avalanche is awesome.)

We were very lucky that the weather was clear so the views from the top of Erebus were superb. The air in Antarctica is very pure and clear so once we were on high ground, we could see enormous distances. We must have been able to see well over 250 kilometres. To the south, the Ross Ice Shelf, or 'Barrier' as Ross called it, stretched away as a great white plain. It might have been a 'barrier' to Ross in his ships, but to us it would be a smooth highway to start our journey to the Pole. To the east behind Mount Terror, the cliffs marking the edge of the Ice Shelf marched away towards the Bay of Whales and the site of Amundsen's base, Framheim. To the west and below us was the Hut Point peninsula with McMurdo and Scott Base at the end. Beyond that we could see McMurdo Sound, named by Ross after the First Lieutenant of his ship, the 'Terror'. In the distance, along the western horizon, were the Trans-Antarctic mountains. To the north was the Ross Sea, filled to the horizon with pack-ice and icebergs. We wondered where the Southern Quest was.

You do not linger at nearly 3800 metres on top of a still-active volcano, so we circled round the crater and descended on skis towards Mount Terra Nova. We camped in the col between the mountains. We only had one two-man tent with us so we had to take turns spending the night outside in a bivouac bag. I have never felt so cold as I did in that bag; I wore a down jacket and trousers and my boot inners but because we were travelling light we only had the inner sleeping bags, not our full double bags. It was a relief to get moving the next day to take in Mount Terra Nova. The weather held out and on the third day we climbed to the top of Mount Terror. From here we were able to look down on Cape Crozier where the Ice Shelf juts out past the eastern tip of Ross Island. It was to Cape Crozier that Wilson, Bowers and Cherry-Garrard, of the Scott expedition, came in 1911 to search for emperor penguin eggs. We determined we would do the same journey later in the winter.

Safe return

From the summit of Mount Terror we quickly descended to the Ice Shelf. We found an American hut at the bottom of the mountain in which we rested for a couple of days before starting for home. Going back on the Ice Shelf was more direct but the surfaces in the region called the Windless Bight were very soft and slow. We arrived at Scott Base after six days travelling. We had been able to carry only seven days food with us so we were glad to get back in time.

By now, it being early April, the sea in McMurdo Sound had started to freeze over, but the ice was not thick enough to be safe to cross so we had to negotiate the rocks and crevasses of an overland journey back to Cape Evans.'

The sea-ice was not reliably safe to travel on until nearly the end of May. Sea-ice is stronger, centimetre for centimetre, than fresh water ice. Sea-ice is more elastic, no doubt something to do with the salt in it, so less likely to snap. We decided that 15 centimetres would be thick enough, especially for someone on skis which would spread the weight. But thickness does not guarantee safety, as the ice is vulnerable to being blown out to sea by strong winds. Two men had died on one of Shackleton's expeditions when, on 10 May 1916, the ice they were travelling on between Hut Point and Cape Evans was blown out to sea where it broke up and they were drowned. The thought of their horror as they realized what was happening was a deterrent for us. So we waited until the ice had successfully withstood a gale.

By the end of May we were happy that the sea-ice was going to be stable for the rest of the winter. The first people to venture out on it were Roger and Mike who in typically eccentric British fashion decided to bicycle to McMurdo – 'to give the Americans a surprise'! (We were not the first people to take bicycles to the Antarctic – Griffith Taylor had taken one in 1911.) When the Americans saw lights weaving and flashing out on the ice, they thought there must be Martians out there. Some ran for shelter and some ran for guns – but it was all right, only two 'Brits' on bikes with lights on to avoid bumping into any unsuspecting Weddell seals.

Map showing the route of the first journey made by Roger, Gareth and Mike over Mount Erebus and Mount Terror. Also shown is their later Winter Journey to Cape Crozier.

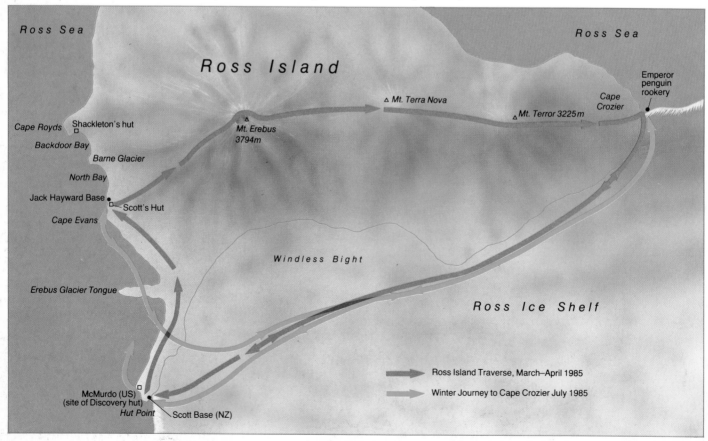

Midwinter and the 'Worst Journey'

We celebrated Midwinter's Day with the greatest possible style. John and Mike were up early baking mince pies and cakes and soon the rest of us were up decorating the hut with all our flags. The high point of the day was the dinner. This was to be a five course affair and we started with shrimps and smoked salmon, followed by pâté, roast chicken (which we had kept frozen in a snow-drift since our arrival), mince pies, and Christmas pudding and brandy butter. Finally, Christmas cakes, sent to us by friends, and cheese finished off both the meal and us. It was all washed down with ample wine of various sorts. We also took part in a more recent tradition of sending greetings telegrams to all the other Antarctic bases.

As we sat in replete silence, I thought with a shiver of anticipation of the Sun now starting to climb back into southern skies, bringing the summer with it and the prospect of the 1500 kilometre march to the South Pole.

Captain Scott's last birthday party.
Left to right: Atkinson, Meares, Oates (standing), Cherry-Garrard, Taylor, Nelson, 'Teddy' Evans, Scott, Wilson, Simpson, Bowers, Gran (standing), Wright, Debenham, Day.

Midwinter's Day feast at Jack Hayward Base. Left to right: Mike, Roger, me, Gareth, John.

In the Antarctic, Midwinter's Day (21 June) fulfils the role of both Christmas and New Year. Scott called it the 'High Festival Of Midwinter' and certainly all expeditions to the Antarctic observe it. It is the shortest day in the southern hemisphere but at our latitude it was more like the longest night. We had not seen the Sun since 12 April and since mid-May it had been dark for 24 hours a day.

In these circumstances the Moon makes an enormous difference as it appears on its regular orbit round the Earth. At full Moon with a clear sky we could see Hut Point, 27 kilometres away. Moonlight there is almost like daylight as the snow effectively doubles the amount of light by reflecting it. Even without the Moon, the light from the stars on a clear night makes it possible to stumble about outside. But if it is cloudy and there is no Moon, it is as black as pitch.

The Aurora

One of the special features of winter in the polar regions is the Aurora. In the Antarctic it is called the Aurora Australis and in the Arctic, the Aurora Borealis. These are Latin words: Australis and Borealis mean south and north respectively; Aurora means 'dawn'. The effect is also called the Southern or Northern Lights. The early explorers thought that these lights were like the

Previous page: The Aurora Australis.

dawn, even though they go on all night. People have always watched the Auroras with awe; the shimmering, flickering, ever-changing curtains, arcs and beams, sometimes in reds and greens, sometimes a mysterious silver, do not seem to be part of this world. Even the usually down-to-earth Captain Scott wrote: 'Might not the inhabitants of some other world controlling mighty forces thus surround our globe with fiery symbols, a golden writing which we have not yet the key to discover?'

Even as early as 1911, scientists had associated the Aurora with sunspot activity and were hot on the track of what we know now, namely, that it is caused by charged particles, streaming from the Sun, which glow when they encounter the Earth's magnetic field and are attracted towards one or the other of the Earth's magnetic poles. (The magnetic poles do not coincide with the geographical poles but move up to 1500 kilometres away. Explorers have been almost as interested in them as in the geographical poles because of their importance in understanding how navigational compasses work.)

Keeping fit
Scott's party used to go for brisk walks with their ponies and dogs to keep fit in the winter. We indulged in the modern equivalent – jogging. The surface was not ideal and I dreaded twisting an ankle, but the feeling of movement and freedom

Bowers, Wilson and Cherry-Garrard before setting out on the Winter Journey to Cape Crozier.

was wonderful after the cramped conditions in the hut.

There were a number of Weddell seals sharing the beach with us. They were our only close neighbours during the winter. They would haul up on to the beach and lie in a wheezy sleep, whatever the weather, sometimes being partially buried by drifting snow. On one of my runs I inadvertently trod on one, thinking it was a smooth rock. I do not know who was more surprised, but despite what I imagine is a rare occasion for a seal, after the initial commotion it soon dropped off back to sleep again, probably thinking it had had a nightmare!

Winter Journey
A week after Midwinter, Roger, Mike and Gareth set out to retrace the Winter Journey to Cape Crozier undertaken by Wilson, Bowers and Cherry-Garrard in 1911. The purpose of the journey in 1911 was to collect some emperor penguins' eggs. At that time there was a theory held among biologists that the key to evolution could be found in the successive stages an

Emperor penguins and their chicks. The picture was taken in the spring after the return of the Sun.

embryo went through. (That theory has now been found to be false.) Wilson thought that emperor penguins' embryos might be particularly interesting, and after five weeks of the most awful struggle they returned with three eggs. They had endured temperatures as low as −60°C and winds up to 160 kilometres per hour. They built a stone igloo to live in whilst they were there. The canvas roof blew off and so they spent a day and a half exposed to the blizzard.

The modern-day journey also met with some testing times during their 30 days away, particularly as the temperature dropped to −54°C. The average was in the −40s. All the equipment performed well but, despite the best clothing money could buy, they also came near to frost-bite on several occasions. It was most unfortunate that the party could not find the main emperor penguin rookery, only a few juveniles. What they did find, though, was the remains of

the hut the pioneers had built all those years ago. It was a touching moment and as Mike said later 'we almost expected three shadowy figures to appear out of the murk'.

They had a lucky escape while out looking for the penguins. It was the moment all explorers dread; being cut off from shelter by deteriorating weather. Fortunately, Roger was able to get a compass bearing on the hut they were staying in before it actually disappeared in the whirling snow, so they found it all right. If he had not been experienced and not got a bearing, their bodies could be out there still. It is vital to know where you are in relation to your shelter, hut or tent, at all times.

It was on the way back that they were caught by the very low temperatures. After exposure (hypothermia), where the body core gets so chilled it cannot function, frost-bite is the greatest danger when it is very cold. Frost-bite is simply a part of the skin freezing. It usually happens to the face first and then the extremities, ie. the hands and feet, where the circulation is not so good. The first warning of approaching frost-bite is numbness of the afflicted part. If it does not soon give way to the most frightful 'heat pains' as the circulation is restored, it is time to stop, put up the tent and have a hot drink while the numb part is warmed up in a warm place — usually in a friend's arm-pit! If fingers or toes are allowed to get frozen for any length of time, the frozen skin cells will die because the blood cannot circulate through the frozen bit. Then the victim may lose the fingers or toes. Frost 'nips' on the face, especially on the nose, are quite common at that sort of temperature, but if the group is vigilant and warn each other if a frozen, white spot appears on someone's face, it can easily be

thawed with a warm hand and no damage is done. It says a lot for our clothing and the party's expertise that, despite these temperatures, no one was frost-bitten.

Perhaps the most useful result of the trip was that they found that the sledges that Roger had designed were ideal. We would therefore take them on the journey to the Pole.

Cherry-Garrard called the 1911 journey 'The Worst Journey in the World', and after our party's experiences, we could see why. But our admiration for those men who could endure such an ordeal without forgetting simple politeness to each other, reached new heights.

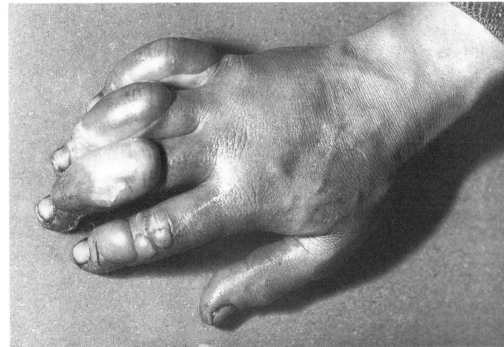

Surgeon Atkinson's frost-bitten hand. This photograph was taken on 5 July, 1911, when Atkinson had been found by a search party after he lost his way in a blizzard. He was missing for about 6 hours, and, although at first less than 500 metres from the hut, he wandered about 7 kilometres in the wrong direction.

Michael's frost-bitten fingers. Where the flesh has been frozen it comes up in blisters. This happened when he was making a solo winter ascent of Mount Erebus.

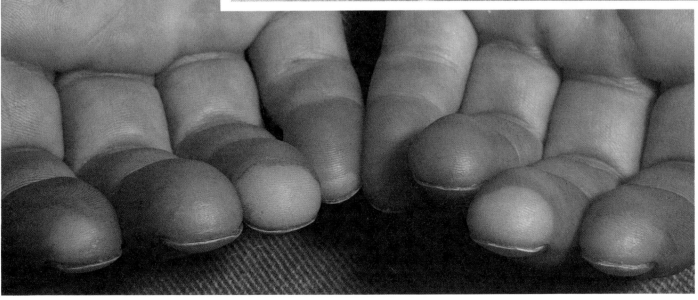

Preparations for the Polar Journey

After the winter, the worst thing was having to make the decision who was going to be the third member of the South Pole party. Roger and I had originally planned that only two of us would walk to the South Pole. After much discussion, we had later decided that the party should have three members; this would not only be safer but would spread the loads over three sledges. The question was – who would be the third member? John did not want to do it, and he had his film to make, so the choice was between Mike and Gareth. Both had excellent qualifications and both wanted to go. It was awful having to decide. Eventually we plumped for Gareth. He was a good navigator and, more importantly, he had been a climbing friend of Roger's, and we thought that this would help reduce the inevitable stresses of the journey.

Unwrapping Yorkie bars before packing them in the sledges. The total weight of all the papers was 737 grams.

Opposite: Weddell seal and pup.

Left to right: John, me, Gareth, Michael and Roger with the contents of one of the sledges.

The Cape Crozier party returned on 28 July, just as we started to get a bit of twilight. We intended to start the journey to the Pole on 26 October so that gave us three months to put the lessons learned from the Winter Journey into practice. There was also the food to calculate, weigh out and pack.

In a small hut like ours, with five of us living on top of each other, it was only to be expected that we got on each other's nerves to a certain extent. We were all suffering from anxiety about this major journey ahead of us, which was made worse by the knowledge that back home there were hundreds of people supporting us in one way or another and relying on us to get to the Pole and make a success of the expedition. It was not an easy time. But when the Sun returned on 22 August, and the beach and the hut were ablaze with light, the world seemed a brighter, more cheerful place and we all suddenly felt optimistic. We were going to the South Pole!

Springtime

The spring was lovely. The weather was good and the Sun shone most days. Out on the sea-ice, Weddell seals were having their pups. The pups were charming little brown creatures with big, black, watery eyes. They always lay very close to their mothers, but, if you were very quiet, you could creep up and give one a little tickle. They were very trusting and would lie there giving little

Gareth and I packing a sledge in the hut. Each packet contained most of one day's food.

bleats and wriggles. We had to be careful not to wake mother – she might not have much in the way of teeth, but she could give us a nasty suck!

Later on, the Adelie penguins started to visit us again, so we knew that they had returned to their rookery at Cape Royds. They cruised about in small gangs like dapper little thugs. If they saw us, they would hurry towards us calling to each other with harsh 'caws'. About five metres away, they would stop and goggle at you, raising and lowering their heads and peeking out of one eye and then the other. Then they would puff themselves up to make themselves look bigger than their half-metre high bodies actually were. Even if we walked towards them, they would hold their ground till the last minute before finally losing their nerve and running away. But they

would not go back into the sea. Their deadliest enemy, the leopard seal, lives out there, patrolling the waters off the rookery and looking for a meal.

I hated the thought of the possibility of all this being destroyed. For the Antarctic wildlife, it is a harsh enough struggle to survive as it is. If the efforts of people, perhaps striving to make an extra dollar from extracting oil, should cause some accident, the consequences would be catastrophic. We have a duty to the other occupants of our planet to protect them from human errors.

Antarctic mail
Spring meant the arrival of post, once more. There is no regular mail delivery in Antarctica – no postman plodding round the bases. Each country brings its own as and when a ship or plane comes in from the outside world. Ours mostly came in via the New Zealand base.

Departure

Time passed quickly and pleasantly. But the spectre of the approaching journey – 1500 kilometres across the Antarctic – was always looking over our shoulders. Besides, we had to avenge the five lives lost on the Scott expedition – we must make it. Roger and Gareth started the preparations. The priority was to cut to a minimum the weight we had to pull. Roger started by cutting out the strengthening bars in the sledges. We then sat down one evening and took the wrappings off every single bar of chocolate, that was a quarter kilo less for each of us to pull! By the time we had finished, we had got our starting weight reduced to 160 kilos each. We would reduce that by a kilo a day, as we ate the food, but it was still a lot to pull.

Scott left Cape Evans at the start of his Polar journey on 26 October and we determined to do the same. On the 25th, I visited Scott's hut for the last time. I lay down on Scott's bunk, and looked at the ceiling and I felt that his spirit was present. Before I left, I went to each bunk and said goodbye to each of the other four – Wilson, Bowers, Oates and Evans. And then I walked out of the hut. I will meet your spirits again out there, I thought.

First steps

It only took a day to get across the sea-ice to McMurdo. We camped near Scott's first 'Discovery' hut, and then round to Scott Base the next day. Then the blizzard struck. It seemed a waste of precious supplies to camp next to our friends at the Base, so we retired to the buildings.

What was going on? Six days later, the weather cleared to hazy sunshine, ragged low cloud, and spindrift pouring off the edge of the Ice Shelf in front of the windows. It was time to go but why had the weather held us up until the precise anniversary date of Scott's departure? It was on 3 November 1911 that Scott left the 'Discovery' hut. He wrote in his diary, 'Camp 1. A keen wind with some drift at Hut Point, but we sailed away in detachments.'

We only had one detachment, no ponies, no dogs, no-one else. Like Scott, we did not carry a radio – we wanted to be completely self-reliant – so it would not be possible to call for help if the going got rough. Just the three of us were going to walk to the South Pole through 1500 kilometres of the most hostile environment in the world. And we were going to make it.

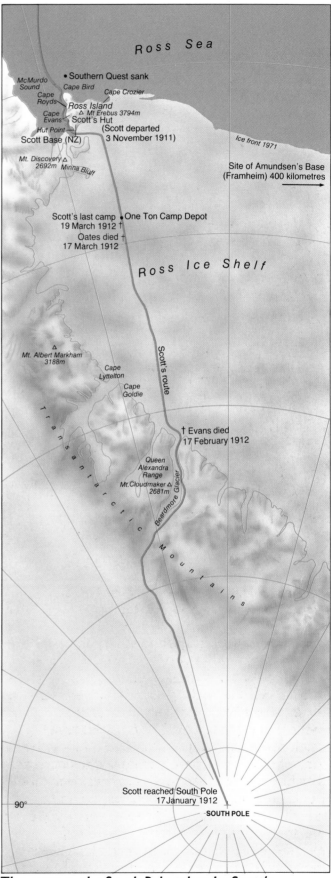

The route to the South Pole taken by Scott's expedition in 1911–12, and followed by our 'In the Footsteps of Scott' expedition in 1985–86.

29

Across the Ice Shelf

Mike and John accompanied us for the first three days, principally so John could film us in action; sledging, making camp, and so on. Rather than use a video camera, he had gone for the full works with a 16mm professional camera. He said he did not mind the extra weight because, after all, there was going to be only one opportunity on this bit so it had to be good. I wondered how we would look on film! When they left us on 6 November, it was an emotional event. Their support and best wishes carried us forward with a spring in our step.

Can you imagine the Ice Shelf? 650 kilometres of absolutely flat, white nothing, that is, a distance equivalent to that from London to Edinburgh. Mount Erebus, with its great plume of steam and cloud was behind us. It must have made a wonderful beacon to Scott's supporting parties returning to Cape Evans. Those men were tough; they man-hauled their sledges for over 2500 kilometres! Soon Minna Bluff and Mount Discovery were behind us and to the side, we could see nothing but a white plain. With little on Earth to look at, I began to take a great interest in the clouds. We must have been able to see the higher clouds, particularly the beautiful wispy cirrus, over 150 kilometres away in any direction. The skyscape dominates the landscape. 650 kilometres to the Beardmore Glacier – Shackleton's and Scott's 'Gateway' to the South Pole.

Above: Our tent after a blizzard. The snow piles up on the leeward side of a tent as the wind eddies round it.

Opposite: Mount Erebus from the Ross Ice Shelf. Our hut was at its base on the other side. The top of the mountain was visible up to 150 kilometres away.

Each day was the same. The alarm went at 7.00 am and one of us got up to light the stove for breakfast. We had to have an alarm; we were getting so tired that without it we would have slept until midday.

Food

Breakfast was hot chocolate, biscuits, butter and oatmeal blocks. Then we got up, stuffed away our sleeping bags, cleared out the tent, collapsed it, packed the sledges, put on our skis, and set off. Once we had finished breakfast, we had to move quickly or else we would have got cold. We set off taking it in turns to lead, three hours at a time. Navigation was simple; we had chosen a direct route once we were past Minna Bluff and all its crevassing. We knew our compass bearing. The person leading stopped and sighted periodically on a distant distinctive patch of snow or even part of a cloud and then walked towards it, pausing now and then to check. At the end of three hours, the leader stopped and the others caught up, and we had a hot drink from the Thermoses. Then another three hours and a stop for lunch. That was soup, biscuits, butter, salami and chocolate. I used to save my two bars to eat at once after supper – the others would eat theirs bit by bit during the day. As I ate mine, the others would watch like hungry dogs, but then they would get their own back during the day. But I liked mine when the warmth in the tent had softened it a bit: from the consistency of granite . . . to marble! We needed all the energy we could get so we ate lots of fat . . . including a quarter kilo of butter a day! We had worked out supplies for a 5,100 calories-a-day diet but still lost weight on the journey – but disproved the theories of experts who had said we would need 8000 calories per day.

At each stop, we looked anxiously at the meters on the sledge wheels. Ours were super high-tech lightweight wheels with accurate and, above all, reliable meters. One revolution of the wheel meant two metres nearer the Pole. The compass and sledge-wheel combination gave us our 'dead-reckoning' position. Once we were up the glacier on to the polar plateau, then we would start to take the Sun sights with the sextant that gave us an accurate position.

Three more hours after lunch and we stopped for 'tea'. Alas no tea, only more chocolate. Tea bags are heavy and do not give any calories, so we had to do without. And then on for another hour before making camp. We had to make an average of 16 kilometres a day in order to reach the South Pole in 90 days. That was all we had food for. But we also had to conserve our energy, we must take it easy and not rush during these early days. We started with our sledges weighing 160 kilos, and you cannot rush that sort of weight along!

Right: Gareth checking the sledge wheel. You can see the yellow box with the window where the figures show.

Below: Inside their tent: left to right, Edgar Evans, Bowers, Wilson and Scott.

Tedium

And so the days went past. On 14 November, eleven days out from Scott Base, we passed the 160 kilometre mark. We skied along, the conversation long since dried up. Talking makes you thirsty and skiing was already thirsty work. Each one of us was wrapped up in his own thoughts. The tedium of skiing along with nothing to look at was indescribable. To overcome it, I used to walk in my imagination through the streets of London. One day, it would be from Westminster to the City, another from Piccadilly to the King's Road. The only trouble with this was that when I imagined passing a restaurant, I would immediately start thinking of food, and I would wonder what was on the menu! We were always hungry.

The worst bit of all was leading in a white-out. Out there, it would happen easily. A layer of low featureless cloud blots out the Sun and the light seems to go dead, with no shadows to show any changes in the ground surface. The sky and the snow merge and there is no horizon. The feeling

All five of us line up for a team photo before John and Mike left us to return to Cape Evans.

was of walking inside a ping-pong ball and it was very tiring. We had only the compass to give us a sense of direction, and sometimes we began to doubt that.

On 16 November we reached the site of One Ton Depot, and on 17 November, 18 kilometres on, the site of Scott's last camp. Of course, all these places have been moving position steadily towards the sea with the ice, but it is the feel of the site which counts. I had been expecting, in my imagination, to see the huge cairn the Search Party built over the bodies, surmounted with a cross made from skis. The place was empty but the spirit was there.

Gareth and I both started to suffer with sore feet, and we had to devote time and attention to looking after them in the evenings. Our feet were desperately important in succeeding and we had to look after them. Fortunately mine healed but unluckily Gareth's did not, and he suffered agony.

On 26 November, we saw solid 'land' again; the mountains of the Queen Alexandra Range. Soon we would be able to see the Beardmore Glacier. What a relief it was to have something to rest the eyes on. I felt as if we had crossed an important psychological barrier.

The only book we had was Scott's diary, and every day we read the entry for the same day in 1911. Scott did not see land until 28 November:

'The land showed up late yesterday; Mount Markham, a magnificent triple peak, appearing wonderfully close, Cape Lyttelton and Cape Goldie.' A few days later, Scott was caught in a blizzard and was tent-bound for five days. Even at this early stage it set the seal on his fate. He started on to the Beardmore Glacier on 10 December, and so did we, but we had a nasty surprise waiting for us.

Captain Scott in April 1911. The Nansen type of sledge was named after Fridtjof Nansen, the Norwegian explorer who invented it. It was made of wood, ours were made of Kevlar. Compare Captain Scott's clothes with ours (see page 18). His were made from cotton and wool which absorbed sweat, making them damp and cold, and also heavy. He is wearing wolfskin mitts and reindeer skin boots which were stuffed with a special sort of grass. Our clothing was mostly made from artificial fibres which did not absorb sweat so were warmer and lighter.

On the sledge, at the front, is a sleeping bag (made out of reindeer skin and not very warm), and on top you can see the tent poles. Scott used a pyramid-type of tent which was very strong, though heavy. Ours was a dome-type, specially designed and made for the expedition.

The Beardmore Glacier

Once on the glacier, we started to climb. Thank goodness our sledges were lighter. Roger led on the first stage so he could take some photographs of us following, and as I approached him, I could tell there was something wrong. As I came closer, I noticed something beyond him, something that did not look natural. I blinked and squinted against the light – it was a helicopter and some tents. Other people! I could have wept. How could we recapture the spirit of nearly 75 years ago if there were helicopters and people about with radios and things. But what could we do except bow to the inevitable? This was 1985, after all. So we walked over to them and said hello.

They were a party of American and Russian geologists, just three of them. They were very welcoming and we spent two days in their company living on steaks and lobster tails! The American Antarctic explorers live well! At last, on 13 December, we said goodbye to Ron, Scott and Eugene, and set off up the glacier.

Later that day, we passed the site where Petty Officer Edgar Evans died. I had been loaned his Polar Medal, and at this point, I took it out from where I had sewn it into my jacket. He was the first to die, and it was a great shock to Scott and the others as Evans was the strongest man in the party. We took a poignant photograph of the spot, and carried on.

Above: Scott's polar party on the trail. Left to right: Edgar Evans, Oates, Wilson and Scott. The amount of frost on their faces shows how cold it was.

Previous page: On the glacier. Sun's rays, split up by minute ice crystals, produce the colours (iridescence) in the cirro-cumulus clouds.

The Beardmore Glacier is a river of ice which sweeps down through a gap in the Trans-Antarctic Mountains. The mountain chain forms an effective dam round the great mass of ice of the central polar plateau, but there are several places where the dam 'leaks', and the Beardmore is one of them. It was first discovered by Shackleton in 1908, and he named it after his benefactor, Sir William Beardmore. It is over 190 kilometres long, starting at a height of 3000 metres and ending in the Ross Ice Shelf at sea level.

Scott followed Shackleton's pioneering route, just as we followed Scott's. The bottom of the glacier is a mass of tumbled blocks of ice and crevasses as it breaks up under its own pressure pushing against the Ice Shelf. By a stroke of luck,

Shackleton found a way through this which he called 'The Gateway'.

Injuries

We had much better surfaces than Scott did, including several stretches of bare ice. Poor Scott had to climb through knee deep, porridge-like snow. With crampons on, and using ski poles for balance and extra grip, we made good progress. At one point, I twisted my knee as my sledge bounced off a rough bit. The others were far ahead and I limped on painfully. I felt dreadfully lonely and vulnerable. We were approaching the point of no return . . . if any accident happened before then, we could still turn back, but once past that point, we had to push on to the Pole, despite the harsh conditions on the plateau. This accident to my knee and Gareth's feet worried me immensely. The rough jarring of crampons on ice did not help at all, and we both looked forward to getting on to our skis again for a smoother ride.

On 16 December we passed under Mount Cloudmaker. What a good name that is — you just cannot miss it with the clouds gathered round its summit. We spent the next few days camping out without the tent. The weather was glorious – flat calm, 24 hours sunshine per day, and in the most glorious scenery.

Crevasses

Crevasses are the big danger on the glacier. Where the ice is bare, they can be seen and there is little danger, but when the snow covers them, forming a 'bridge', they become really dangerous because the crevasses are hidden. Sometimes we could see the bridges as sunken patches and sometimes we couldn't. When we could see the bridges, we could test how thick they were so we did not fall through. (A bridge should be at least 2 metres thick to be safe.) But there was still the possibility of the whole bridge collapsing under the extra weight. We had to rope together to pass over these, so if one of us fell, the other two could hold him up and help him out. But generally, Roger was very good at finding bridges, testing them and guiding us across.

On 22 December, we were under 480 kilometres from the South Pole and on the 23rd, we reached the polar plateau at last. We were 3150 metres above sea level there, and surprisingly, it was downhill to the Pole which is 300 metres lower.

Cross-section of a crevasse showing the snow bridge which can be a trap. But this one looks thick enough to support someone's weight.

Above: Looking along an open crevasse.
Below: Aerial view of heavy crevassing on a glacier flowing from right to left.

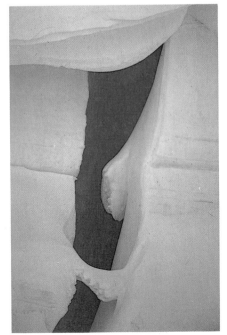

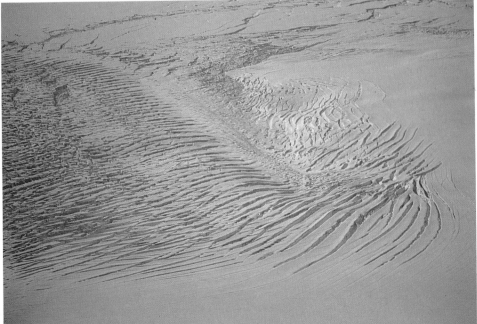

Across the Plateau to the Pole

On 24 December, my mind started to turn increasingly to thoughts of home. I wondered if they were having a white Christmas! There were no problems here on that score, only a lack of Christmas trees! Christmas Day brought us 25 kilometres nearer the Pole, and at the end of the day, an enormous feast with double quantities of everything. As a surprise, Roger suddenly produced two teabags. It tasted like the best drink in the world – so refreshing and thirst-quenching. We had brew after brew of tea until, after six mugs, we decided we were actually drinking water!

On 28 December, we were 320 kilometres from the Pole and we were getting more and more excited. Everything was going well; we had plenty of food and the surfaces were getting better and better. I think we all were calculating in our minds when we were going to arrive at the Pole. Only 13 more days to go! But the fly in the ointment was the wind. It was what Scott would call 'a searching wind'; it searched out every little chink in the armour of our clothing. It must have been hell up there for Scott and his men, with their poor clothing and inadequate rations.

Above: Sastrugi. Strong winds have carved these waves in the snow. They form parallel to the direction of the wind.

Opposite: Roger using the sextant. He is sighting on the Sun's reflection in the artificial horizon, which is in the box on the snow. You have to do this if there is no level horizon like there is at sea.

From the top of the glacier, we were crossing another featureless plain. We started to use the sextant to find out our position. 320 kilometres away was the small cluster of huts that marks the South Pole. (The Americans built a base there in 1959 with everything flown in from McMurdo, at phenomenal cost.) We were aiming for that base.

Getting our bearings

The sextant is a traditional navigation device. Although now being superseded by electronic satellite navigation, the sextant is simple and reliable but it is fragile and must be looked after. All it does is measure angles, particularly the angle formed by the height of the Sun. We took our 'sight' when the Sun is at its highest at midday, and then referred to some tables in a book, to find out the latitude. We only needed to know our latitude, so that we could aim for 90 degrees south, the latitude of the South Pole.

We had another celebration on 31 December, with only 240 kilometres to go. That was the day we hit the first sastrugi of the polar plateau. We had been expecting it and it was only a minor inconvenience at that stage. Sastrugi is a Russian word for a snow surface carved by the wind into furrows and ridges. The ridges are highly irregular and can vary in size from a few centimetres to half a metre high or more. It slowed us down a bit, but it made travelling more interesting. Some of the shapes were fantastic.

It was much colder up there and we had to start being careful about frost-bite again. We had to be quick taking gloves off . . . think about what we wanted to do, whip off a glove, do the job and hurry the glove on again. Some metal things, particularly aluminium, are bad to touch. Your fingers stick to it and can burn you like heat.

Scott's party at the South Pole, 18 January 1912. The strain of hauling the sledges and the demoralization of being beaten by Amundsen is evident in their faces. Left to right: Oates, Bowers (seated), Scott, Wilson (seated), Edgar Evans.

Arrival at the Pole! Gareth and I pulling our sledges towards the American Amundsen-Scott Base.

Arrival at the Pole

On 4 January, we were 160 kilometres from the Pole, with only a week's more walking. We had plenty of food and fuel in hand. I could hardly bear the anticipation. It was cold and windy, temperatures below −20°C, with a head wind. It made for unpleasant sledging. Despite the sastrugi, we were making 24 kilometres a day. The surface was much harder there and the skins under the skis gripped much better. We were all extremely fit.

On 7 January, 83 kilometres to go, on the 8th, 59 kilometres − only two days to go. On 9 January, we made only 16 kilometres as the visibility was cut. It was there that 'Birdie' Bowers had spotted the black flag which warned them they had been pipped to the Pole by Amundsen. Dog foot prints in the snow had confirmed who it was.

On 10 January, with less than 26 kilometres to go, we totted up our supplies: we still had food for nearly three weeks and fuel for a month. But were we in fact only 26 kilometres away? We had not seen any signs indicating other humans nearby.

On 11 January, we set out despite a strong wind with heavy drifting snow. We later found that the wind was the strongest ever recorded at the South Pole − 59 kph − which with a temperature of −30°C gave a 'windchill factor', or equivalent temperature, on exposed flesh of −62°C. We managed nearly 6 kilometres but the wind got stronger and stronger and the snow was whipped up until we could barely see 10 metres. It was so frustrating to have to stop so close to our goal. We could not march on a compass bearing, because the Earth's magnetic field is too weak there and the needle wobbles uselessly. So we put up the tent and got into our sleeping bags to keep warm. The only book we had with us was Scott's Diary, and I looked up to see what he was doing on 10 January 1912' . . . Terrible hard march in the morning; only covered 5.1 miles . . . Only 85 miles (geo.) from the Pole, but it's going to be a stiff pull both ways apparently; still we do make progress which is something.'

Four hours later, the wind had dropped sufficiently to enable us to make a move. After a further two hours sledging, I spotted an object off to one side poking up above the still drifting snow. This became clearer as a meteorological tower with a flag line leading away, presumably to the

The Southern Quest going down, crushed by pack-ice closing in on her. Pack-ice is accumulated old and new frozen sea water. It can reach 3 or 4 metres thick and when driven by winds and currents can exert immense force.

Pole itself. We followed this, still unable to see much about us for the drifting snow. Then – there! There it was! Above the flickering snow was the top of a dome, the geodesic dome that covers the American base. We set off again at a great pace, but infuriatingly it did not seem to get any nearer for ages because visibility is so good in the pure clear air.

At last, we could see the entrance. A heavily clothed figure came out and walked past us, looked at us and walked on. A few paces later, he stopped and looked again. 'Hey, the Footsteps are here!' We had made it. Our sledge-wheel and compass put us less than half a kilometre short and a kilometre out to the east – not bad over nearly 1500 kilometres.

A few hours later, we had our photograph taken by the 'Barber's Pole', which marks the southern point of the Earth's axis – the South Pole. I was standing at the bottom of the world, I felt like a fly on a ceiling, but whirling around at 1600 kph, with my head in space. We had done it – my dream had come true. I had followed in Scott's footsteps, I had felt what it was like to be

Our Cessna in which Giles Kershaw (on the right) was going to fly us back from the South Pole.

The great snow cairn raised over the bodies of Scott, Wilson and Bowers, which were found in November 1912.

isolated and totally reliant on myself and only two companions. But above all, we had achieved what we had set out to do. The old saying, 'Where there is a will, there is a way', still held true.

But it was too good to last. The American base commander came up and said, 'I've got some bad news for you guys. Your ship has just sunk off Beaufort Island . . . crushed in the ice, I guess. All the crew are safe though, and a chopper has flown them in to McMurdo.'

We had no communications so I could not find out if Giles Kershaw was coming to collect us in our Cessna. 28 hours after arriving at the Pole, we were being bundled into a Hercules aircraft; the Americans had asked Giles not to fly in to collect us. The dream had collapsed: we were at the mercy of outsiders – farewell independence. The ship's crew could have walked across the pack-ice to Cape Evans. We hated being helped but it is better to be helped than risk lives.

A few hours later, I looked out from the noisy Hercules. Somewhere, 3000 metres below, lay the bodies of Captain Robert Falcon Scott, Royal Navy; Dr Edward Wilson; Captain Oates, Sixth Inniskilling Dragoons; Lieutenant Henry Bowers, Royal Indian Marine; and Petty Officer Edgar Evans, Royal Navy. We had followed the message of their epitaph: 'To strive, to seek, to find and not to yield.'

Epilogue
Roger and I and the crew from the Southern Quest, who were all safe, were flown to New Zealand by the Americans. Gareth stayed on with two volunteers from the Southern Quest to staff

our base until we could raise funds to remove all traces of our having been in Antarctica.

The three men stayed on for another 10 months which were not as uneventful as might have been expected: for political reasons the New Zealanders at Scott Base, and the Americans at McMurdo, were forbidden to have anything to do with the three (Gareth Wood, Steve Broni and Tim Lovejoy) at Jack Hayward Base. Eventually that attitude was relaxed – but only some time after Gareth had had a narrow escape from death.

In April, the three decided to make a journey, before the start of the winter darkness, to Cape Royds and Shackleton's original base. Gareth walked ahead across the sea-ice of Backdoor Bay. He reached a crack which had opened up and then frozen over again with a thin covering of ice. He tapped his boot on the ice to test its strength. Suddenly, he was flat on his back and screaming for help – a ferocious leopard seal, about 4 metres long, had burst through the ice and had locked its jaws around Gareth's leg, dragging him into the crack. Steve ran up and kicked at the seal's head with his cramponed boots. The seal let go abruptly, and Steve and Tim started to drag Gareth away across the ice. But the seal surfaced again and attacked by flinging itself over the ice towards them, grabbing Gareth's boot. Steve kicked out again, this time aiming at the seal's eyes, until it finally let go and Gareth was dragged to safety. It was weeks before Gareth recovered completely.

Meanwhile, the expedition's fund-raising went on and in late December, 1986, Giles Kershaw and I flew across Antarctica in a small, twin-engined Otter aircraft to pick up the three volunteers. We left the Base dismantled and stacked, ready for removal. Before flying out, we cleared up any rubbish so that we left the area as we had found it.

By February 1987, the hut, the Cessna and all the remaining stores and equipment had been taken away by ship: the job was completed. Once again Cape Evans was left to Scott's hut, to the Weddell seals and Adelie penguins . . . their home. Of what had been our home, there was no trace.

A leopard seal displaying its vicious-looking teeth. It was this type of seal which made a ferocious attack on Gareth – the first recorded incident of this kind.

43

Facts About Antarctica

Where is it? Antarctica is at the very bottom of the world, centred about the South Pole.

How big is it? Antarctica is 13.8 million square kilometres in area. That makes it the fifth largest of the seven continents. It is larger than the USA and Mexico combined, and larger than Europe.

How cold is it? The coldest recorded temperature is −89.6°C, recorded at the Russian base Vostok. The warmest recorded temperature at the South Pole is −15°C. The temperatures vary over the rest of the continent; they may rise into positive figures along the Antarctic Peninsula during the summer and, of course, in the sun, temperatures are even higher. But the annual average is below zero everywhere.

How thick is the ice? The greatest recorded depth of ice is 4700 metres. Ice covers 98% of the continent. This also makes it the continent with the highest average height above sea level – of 2250 metres. The annual average accumulation of snow is less than the equivalent of 5 centimetres of rain, which makes it technically a desert so the ice must have built up over millions of years. The highest mountain in Antarctica is Vinson Massif in the Ellsworth Mountains which is 5140 metres high – higher than Mont Blanc in the Alps.

What is the weather like? Apart from being very cold it is also very windy and surprisingly dry. Wind speeds of 320 kph have been recorded. The cold also makes the air very dry. This has a dangerous effect for the people there; most Antarctic bases are built of wood which is cheap and easy to transport as well as being easy to build with. The air dries out the wood making it very easy to catch fire. At least five bases have been burnt down since 1945 and several people have died.

Who lives there? There are no Inuit or other native people there. The only people who live there now are scientists and their assistants and maintenance teams who spend about a year there at any time. In the summer the population is about 2000–3000, living in some 40 bases spread round the continent and the surrounding islands. In winter it drops to about 500 when the scientists go home.

What about the wildlife? There are no native land mammals and there are no polar bears, they live in the Arctic! There are lots of seals: Weddell, crabeater, Ross, leopard and elephant seals and also fur seals, which are technically sea-lions. They all live in the seas around Antarctica and can be seen lying on the pack-ice and on the beaches. There are still quite a lot of whales living in Antarctic waters, not as many as there used to be of course, but now that whaling has all but stopped let us hope that their numbers will start to increase.

Antarctica is famous for its penguins of which there are many species; most common are Adelie, gentoo, chinstrap, macaroni, king and emperor. With the exception of the emperor penguins, they all migrate northwards at the end of the summer. The emperors lay their eggs during the winter. They live in colonies, huddled together for warmth, usually on the sea-ice near the coast. They are therefore Antarctica's only truly resident bird.

Other birds live there in the summer: skuas, gulls, snowy petrels, Wilson's petrels, Antarctic petrels, giant petrels, sheath-bills, Antarctic terns and many types of albatrosses live in the sub-Antarctic islands. The Arctic tern also visits in the summer, thus escaping winter in the Arctic.

A cross-section through Antarctica showing the depth of the ice above the land. At its deepest, it is over 4500 metres thick.

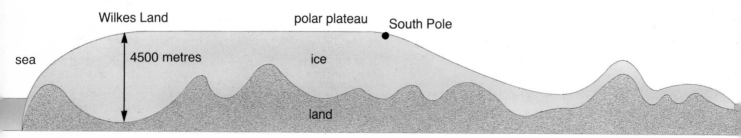

Wilkes Land   polar plateau   South Pole

sea   4500 metres   ice

land

Do any plants grow there? Lichens grow on rocks almost all over the continent, to within 480 kilometres of the South Pole. Mosses are found in more northerly areas, usually in sheltered nooks and crannies facing north towards the Sun. Some very primitive grass grows along the northern shores of the Antarctic Peninsula as far south as 68 degrees latitude. A few insects live in these northerly spots too. There are no flowers, bushes or trees anywhere in Antarctica.

Why is it called Antarctica? The word comes from two Ancient Greek words: *ant*, meaning 'opposite', and *arctos*, which means 'bear'. The Greek word for north was arctos because the constellation 'The Great Bear' is always in the northern sky. 'Arctica' is derived from 'arctos'. Therefore Antarctica means 'opposite to north'.

What is an iceberg? An iceberg is a floating mass of ice. Ice, although just frozen water, is slightly lighter than water so it floats, but about seven eighths are below the surface. Therefore an iceberg showing 30 metres above the water has another 210 metres below the surface. They can vary in size enormously from only a few metres long to tens of kilometres in length. One of the largest on record started off nearly 150 kilometres across. These really big ones are bits of ice-shelves which have broken off. They are soon broken up by waves in the sea and the small ones may be the remains of these monsters, or bits from glaciers which started life much smaller. The process of breaking off from the parent mass is called 'calving'.

What is an ice shelf? An ice shelf, such as the Ross Ice Shelf, or Great Ice Barrier as Scott used to call it, is a floating conglomeration of glaciers. The Ross Ice Shelf is about the size of France and it is actually floating, going up and down with the tides. In places where a glacier meets the ice shelf, the ice may be as much as 900 metres thick, but it is usually less than 300 metres thick at the edge.

What is a crevasse? A crevasse is formed when stresses in the ice have caused it to break. Crevasses most commonly occur on glaciers when the ice flows over an irregularity in the rock underneath. They range in size from a few centimetres wide and deep to tens of metres wide

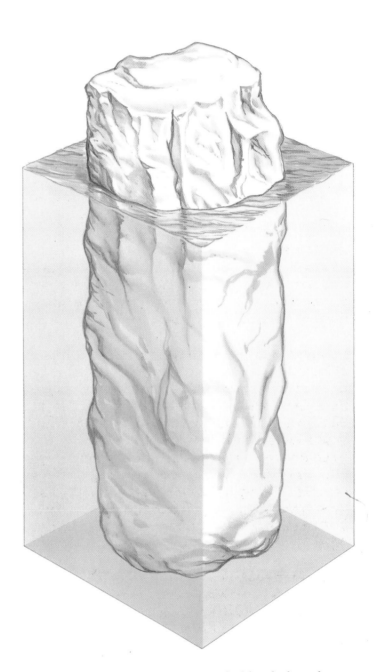

An iceberg, showing the amount hidden below the sea's surface.

and deep. They may also extend for kilometres in length. An average crevasse, if there is such a thing, is about 5 metres wide and 30 metres deep, and about a kilometre long. Crevasses are commonly disguised by a bridge of snow that builds up during the winter. It is a severe test for the explorer to find a crevasse and to make sure that the snow bridge is strong enough to bear a person's weight before venturing across it. Many people have been killed by falling into crevasses.

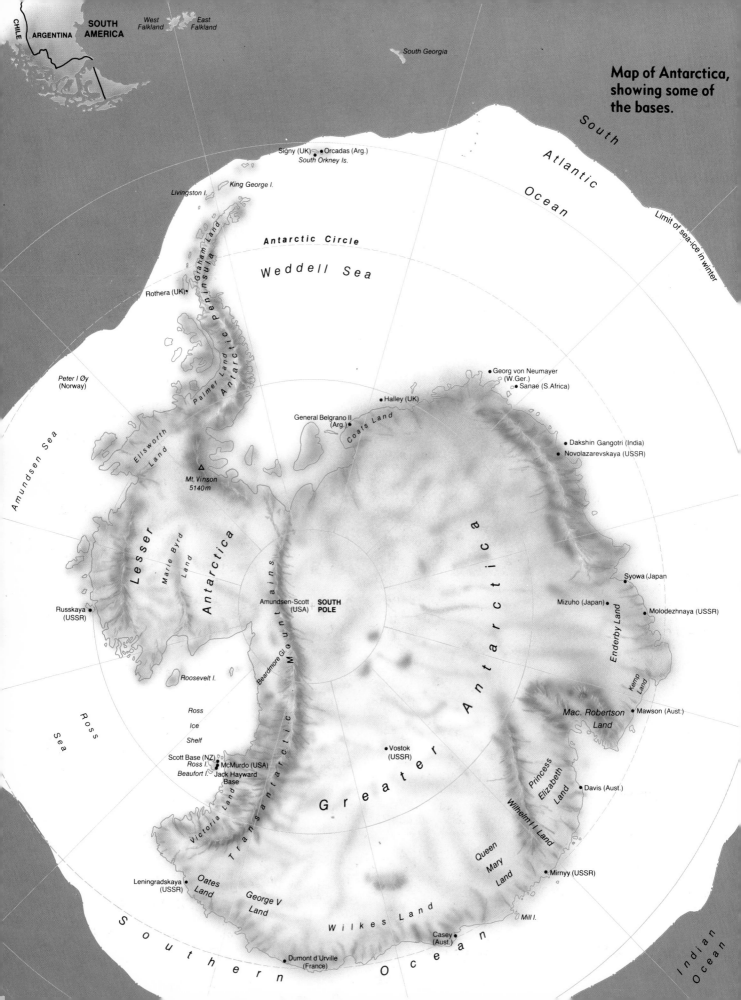

CHILE

ARGENTINA

SOUTH
AMERICA

West
Falkland

East
Falkland

South Georgia

**Map of Antarctica,
showing some of
the bases.**

South

Atlantic

Ocean

Limit of sea-ice in winter

Signy (UK) • • Orcadas (Arg.)
South Orkney Is.

King George I.

Livingston I.

Antarctic Circle

Weddell Sea

Rothera (UK) •

Peter I Øy
(Norway)

Graham Land

Palmer Land

Antarctic Peninsula

Georg von Neumayer •
(W.Ger.)

Sanae (S.Africa) •

Halley (UK) •

General Belgrano II •
(Arg.)

Coats Land

Dakshin Gangotri (India) •
Novolazarevskaya (USSR) •

*Ellsworth
Land*

△ Mt. Vinson
5140m

Amundsen Sea

Lesser

Antarctica

Marie Byrd Land

Russkaya •
(USSR)

Roosevelt I.

*Ross
Ice
Shelf*

Ross

Sea

Scott Base (NZ) •
Ross I. • McMurdo (USA)
Beaufort I. Jack Hayward
Base

Amundsen-Scott
(USA)

**SOUTH
POLE**

Transantarctic Mountains

Beardmore Gl.

Victoria Land

Leningradskaya •
(USSR)

*Oates
Land*

*George V
Land*

G r e a t e r

A n t a r c t i c a

Vostok •
(USSR)

Wilkes Land

Dumont d'Urville •
(France)

Casey •
(Aust.)

Syowa (Japan •

Mizuho (Japan) •
Molodezhnaya (USSR) •

Enderby Land

*Kemp
Land*

*Mac. Robertson
Land*

• Mawson (Aust.)

*Princess
Elizabeth
Land*

Wilhelm II Land

Davis (Aust.) •

*Queen
Mary
Land*

Mirnyy (USSR) •

Mill I.

S o u t h e r n   O c e a n

Indian

Ocean

Index

Page numbers in **bold** refer to illustrations.